© 2000 Clover Stornetta Farms, Inc.

Published by Clover Stornetta Farms
91 Lakeville Street
Petaluma, CA 94952

ISBN: 0-9705718-0-1

Book design: Anne Vernon as
    Benefield, Levinger, McEndy & Vernon
    51 E Street
    Santa Rosa, CA 95404

A QuinnEssentials book
    QuinnEssentials Books & Printing, Inc.
    1370 Industrial Avenue, Suite G
    Petaluma, CA 94952

Printed in Hong Kong through QuinnEssentials

From Left Upper Row: Gary Imm, Lynn Imm, Kevin Imm, John Markusen, Mike Keefer, Anne Benedetti, Dan Benedetti, Herm Benedetti, Paul Ross
From Left Lower Row: Pat Markusen, Evelyn Benedetti, Diane Keefer, Gene Benedetti, Marilyn Benedetti, Lois Ross

Wholly Cow

A historical retrospective of Clo the Cow's billboards

Foreward by Gaye LeBaron
Text by Jim Benefield, Dan Benedetti, and Gene Benedetti
Executive Editor: Anne Vernon

Contributing Billboard Artists:
Gordon Cockroft, Craig Curtiss, Susan Evason, Bill Knight, Lynn Morgan,
Bill Nellor, David Oshiro, Anne Vernon, Jim Wakeman, and Art Zadina

Contributing Billboard Copywriters:
Jim Benefield, Dan Benedetti, John McEndy,
Margo VanMidde, Anne Vernon, and the much appreciated Public

My thanks to the owners: our founder Gene Benedetti and Mom (Evelyn Benedetti),
Gary & Lynn Imm, John & Pat Markusen, Herm & Marilyn Benedetti,
Mike & Diane Keefer, Kevin & Mary Imm, and Paul & Lois Ross (retired).
To our inspiring and loyal customers, thank you with all my heart.

To my wife, Annie, I love you and value your support and love beyond words.

Dan Benedetti

My thanks to Dan Benedetti for his great help, knowledge, and enthusiasm for this project,
Gene Benedetti for creating his extraordinary company and products,
Margo VanMidde for her dedication, thoroughness, chronological research, and support,
Betty Visser for her gracious problem solving and cheerfulness,
the staff of BLM&V for their expertise and attention to detail,
and the public for their great appreciation of our Clo.

Anne Vernon

Foreword

By Gaye LeBaron

What the Big Apple is to New York; what Mickey Mouse is to Anaheim; the koala is to Austraila and Snoopy is to the whole world– that's what Clo the Cow is to California's North Coast.

Our hometown cow makes us laugh, even when we're stuck in traffic. She makes us proud of where we live and reminds us of how kind nature has been to this "chosen spot."

It was the renowned horticulturist Luther Burbank, who first called this place "chosen," and who gave our region its first brush with fame. Burbank would have loved this cow and all she represents.

The strongest link with the past we have in this part of California is the land– the green hills and fertile fields that have produced, and continue to produce, a flourishing agriculture.

Tethered with that thread that ties us to the past is Clo, out there standing in her field, keeping us safe in the knowledge we remain connected to our history.

Her smile is contagious, her puns are outrageous. She is part and parcel of our community.

We all have our favorites. Mine is the cottage cheese board called Clo's Uncownters of the Curd Kind– a rare triple play.

The winning combination of Benedetti, Levinger, Nellor and Benefield have given us a symbol to carry with us into the 21st century. And, who knows, perhaps, the 22nd. It's Clo'ser than you think.

The Beginning

Interview with Jim Benefield, former Chairman of Benefield, Levinger, McEndy & Vernon, who retired in 1995 after 41 years in journalism, public relations and advertising.

For 20 years I carried on a love affair with a chubby-cheeked cutie with pointed ears and big teeth. Her name is Clo, the affable bovine who is everyone's favorite cow. Clo sprang from the pen of Bill Nellor, an art director for Lee Levinger's Santa Rosa ad agency, in 1968. This early rendition looked more like a real cow than the one we know and love today. She wasn't particularly appealing, so in 1969 Bill revised her into a cartoon character that has survived with minor changes for over 30 years. Bill left the agency in 1970, replaced by Chris Alderman at the drawing board.

I bought the ad agency from Lee in 1972, although Lee stayed on to work with Clover for several more years. With Mike Fitzpatrick now doing the artwork, boards such as "Clearly ahead," featuring an inflated likeness of Clo's head bursting through the panel, appeared on Highway 101. For two decades I abandoned conscience to come up with the most outrageous puns I could devise or steal, starting with "Clo's line."

Through the years an outstanding succession of artists have worked on the Clo billboards, including Jim Wakeman, Bill Knight, Craig Curtiss, Susan Evason, David Oshiro, Lynn Morgan, Gordon Cockroft, Anne Vernon, and Art Zadina.

I would like to pontificate about the studies, surveys, blind tastings, copy testing and focus group interviews that contributed to developing a complex marketing strategy for Clover. Unfortunately, because ad men are noted for their humility and candor, I can't. The Clover campaign is based on a couple of obvious points: the client produces an excellent product, and the advertising for something as basic as milk should be kept simple.

Clover advertising in the '50's and early '60's concentrated on building a local image for the dairy — "Aren't you glad you live in Clover Country," featuring scenes of happy young families enjoying Clover Milk in such settings as the redwoods or aboard a Russian River canoe. With the advent of Clo in 1969 this theme became "Support your local cow" and "Local girl makes good," highlighted by the broadly smiling cartoon cow.

Clo was created as a mascot to represent the company, to project a warm, friendly, down home feeling for the dairy and to generate loyalty for its products. That she has succeeded over the last three decades is indicated by the fact that early on she wore a bell around her neck labeled "Clo," so people would know who she was. It would be difficult to find a person in the area today who couldn't identify her. She was chosen one year to be Grand Marshal of Santa Rosa's Rose Parade, and in 1995, the Sonoma County Museum put on a special exhibition tracing her career.

After the "local" boards came a series in a lighter vein, such

"U. F. Clo" at the year 2000 Petaluma Parade–
from the billboard "The New Moollennium" (Page 90)

Clo admires her fleet of moving billboards

as "The Producer," with Clo attired as a Hollywood mogul, complete with dark glasses; "Factory Fresh," with Clo sporting a smokestack; and "The Now Cow," with Clo decked out in psychedelic colors.

The infamous puns came next, starting with "Outstanding in her field" and "Clearly ahead." Two of the favorites came from a 1989 contest for billboard ideas—announced in a message on a milk carton—that attracted 7,481 entries. Top winner, with "Tip Clo through your two lips," was Ally Minatta of Sonoma. Second prize, for "Splendor in the glass," went to Helen Vanderbilt of San Anselmo.

Clo has not been limited to billboards. She shows up in newspaper and magazine ads, school yearbooks and football programs, radio commercials, and an award-winning series of television spots that combined live action with animation to bring three of the billboards to life. A dozen years ago the ad agency embarked on a major redesign project that now features Clo on the packaging for the full line of Clover Stornetta products. And the agency designed an eight-foot, inflatable, walk-around figure of Clo, which appears in parades, store openings and civic events of all kinds. In addition to their roadside locations, the billboards get wide circulation by being painted on the sides of Clover's fleet of trucks.

Through the years the Clover billboards have won a wide array of local, national and international advertising industry awards. The most prestigious recognition came in 1991 when the agency won the top award in the billboard campaign category of the International Advertising Festival of New York, which attracted 3,790 entries from 40 countries. The three boards submitted were "Supreme Quart," with Clo in judicial robes; "Half Galleon," with Clo at sea in pirate garb; and "Splendor in the Glass," with Clo in a flower-filled meadow. Runners-up to the Clover entry were campaigns for Volkswagen, produced by DDB Needham Worldwide of Detroit, and British Aerospace, produced by Austin Knight Advertising Limited of London.

How long can this lighthearted ad campaign go on? As long as Clo continues to bring smiles to the faces of her fans, young and old, and as long as they continue to enjoy the milk lovingly produced by this amiable bovine. There are still plenty of delicious puns in the barrel, eager to

burst forth for the amusement of Clo's friends.

Interview with Gene Benedetti

Chairman of the Board, Gene Benedetti

Chairman of the board and patriarch for Clover Stornetta Farms, interviewed by Anne Vernon

Back around 1951 Lee Levinger came to me in Petaluma and said, "I want to do some advertising for you." He knew that Clover was new in Santa Rosa, and I knew we needed help.

Lee was Clover's first ad man. I had a lot of respect for him because his mind was always going. He became quite a person in Santa Rosa, and in Sonoma County.

He eventually came up with this idea that we should have a billboard. I said, "Lee, you're crazy. Marin County just voted to eliminate billboards. I don't want to make enemies with anybody. Billboards aren't going to be well liked."

Lee said, "I want to do something totally different on a billboard. It will be a series. I want to have a play on words that's going to be very interesting and people are going to anticipate them, and they're going to enjoy them. There will be no hard sell. It will be about happiness, and the good things about Clover. I'm going to develop a cow or something that's a caricature."

So about two-three weeks later he gave me a call. We'd always go to lunch and have a couple martinis, and we'd sit there and shake dice and have a lot of fun, but we'd also conduct business. He had this board, done in freehand himself! And he said, "Now look, this is not the final version of what I want, but I did this, and I'm not an artist. And you can tell as soon as I show it to you that I'm not an artist, but I didn't want to get an artist involved until I could get some kind of approval from you to go ahead with this."

I looked at it and here was a facsimile of Clo–not really the Clo that we have or that we had then even. This was Clo out in a field, and on the top it said "Outstanding in her Field." I liked the idea.

I took it to the Board, put it on the agenda, and I explained what we were doing. One of the board members leaned aside and looked at his secretary. He was an outspoken character and got up and said, "Dammit, Gene, if we're going to have a billboard,–first of all, people don't want billboards now–but if we're going to have a billboard I want a real cow on it!"

I said, "I appreciate your feelings, but we think this is something that will really generate interest." They all sat up, and another one got up and said, "We agree wholeheartedly, we want a real cow."

I said, "You're missing the whole point." But after going round and round, it was finally passed! And the rest is history.

> *"The love between Gene and Lee–they enjoyed each other beyond the business, and it was a wonderful relationship. Clo the cow is like a friendship with the community. It's personal." – Louise Levinger*

Interview with Dan Benedetti

President of Clover Stornetta Farms,
interviewed by Anne Vernon

I have worked in one capacity or another at Clover Stornetta Farms since I was 16. At age 22 my wife Anne and I bought a route and distributed milk in West Marin for five years. Upon the founding of Clover Stornetta Farms in 1977, we became partners.

Prior to 1977 the history of Clover and Stornetta paralled themselves in many ways. Going back to the early 1920's both companies had developed strong local identities in their respective geographical areas. Both were locally owned and operated. Both were in Sonoma County. With Gene Benedetti and Al Stornetta both companies enjoyed strong leadership. Upon the merger of the two well known brands, the name to be used in marketing became a growing concern. We came to realize that both names, Clover-Stornetta, could move this fledgling company forward.

We even had a "Netta, the cow" that we created in 1977. There was a Clo and a Netta. That made perfectly good sense for probably all of two or three weeks, until it became very confusing, and really clouded the whole issue of who this new company, Clover Stornetta Farms, was. We were traditionally known

President Dan Benedetti

as Clo, and Clover country, and now we had a Netta, and Stornetta... it just muddied the water. So we backed up, kept the marketing and corporate name Clover Stornetta Farms, and just left Clo the cow to grow.

We did one billboard, "Mooin' Pitcher Star", that had just the Stornetta carton on it. And now of course, some twenty-three years later, we use the common label, Clover Stornetta.

The billboards were truly an evolutionary phenomenon. We did not strike it rich with "Support your local cow." We didn't have regional, national, or international acclaim with "Local girl makes good," or "Smile, you're in Clover country." But what it did do was set the table for what would later become this growing image of Clover, Clo the cow, and the billboards as something quite unique. It began to institutionalize itself...started to become bigger than life. "Clo's Line" and "Outstanding in her Field" were two early ones that hit it big. And that's when the public began to take ownership.

When Clover Stornetta Farms first came into business, billboards were not a big thing. We couldn't have them in Marin County. That's why we've gone to our trucks. The trucks are our traveling billboards. And they have done quite well for us.

Clo has evolved, the billboards have changed, but as with

everything successful, it took a good strong foundation, and that foundation grew and flourished. Now, it's taken another whole dynamic leap forward in progressive graphics. Some of the ideas now are the most progressive we've seen. More people are looking at them. More people have taken ownership of them, and I think that makes the billboards stronger. The strength of the campaign is that it's taken on a life of it's own through the people.

> *I think there's a part in all of us in society that craves simplicity, and these billboards, silly little puns that they are, sort of ground us all.*

Our challenge as a company, and with our ad agency, is to create something that all people feel close to. If ideas continue to come from the people we will never stray too far from reality. Right now, we know that people have a wonderful time with them.

The strength of Clover Stornetta Farms is much larger than any of us ever dreamt. There are currently seven owners, and we have a following of consumers who keep driving us to perfection, driving us to be what we are today, that's unlike most companies. The phenomenon of Clover is that it's the consumer that has driven this company, not the owners. The owners have guided it, and it's an incredibly loyal consumer base that keeps demanding Clover. It still happens today. We're growing faster than we've ever grown,

again because of the consumer. It's the consumer demand for a product that they realize is better–we think the best in the United States. The cleanest milk in the United States is what we want to produce, and that's what it's all about. Taking care of our communities is equally important. That promotes customer loyalty. Having the best product and the fiercely loyal customer base creates the "people" driven company called Clover Stornetta Farms.

"Clo's Friends"
for the Humane Society

1969-2000

A Retrospective:
31 years of Clo's Billboards

support your
local cow...

buy
Clover
milk

1969

CLOVER
the only milk with
LOVE in it.

THE NOW COW

hours fresher Clover Milk

"THE NOW COW" billboard featured Clo with a hippie headband, attired in the psychedelic colors of the '70s. "The Now Cow," always with it, produced her milk right now, guaranteeing that fresh Clover taste.

1970

FOR GOODNESS SAKE
Drink Clover Milk

1971

country fresh Clover milk Now in town!

Also ran as "It's Great to Live in Clover Country," 1972

1971

This billboard was part of an outdoor and newspaper campaign highlighting the contribution Clover dairy ranches make to preserving the green hills and rural atmosphere of Clover Country. Clover Stornetta Farms remains committed to sustainable agriculture to this day.

1974

"Clo's line" was the first of the long run of pun-driven billboards, each more outrageous than the last.

1976

21

"Outstanding in her field" showed a bell around Clo's neck with her name on it, to help establish name recognition for the lovable bovine early in her career.

Clearly Ahead

"Clearly Ahead" featured an inflated version of Clo's head bursting through the billboard. Shown here are Gene Benedetti and Jim Benefield in front of the Highway 101 board.

Mooin' pitcher star

1982

Clo's
uncounters
of the curd kind

"Clo's uncounters of the curd kind" featured an athletic running Clo, an image that later was used on the packaging for Clover's low-fat products.

Say cheese!
And smile.

Clover-Stornetta
Farms

1984

Supreme Quart

The headline for "Supreme Quart" came from Jim Miller, driver of one of Clover's 40-foot tractor-trailers.

1985

1986

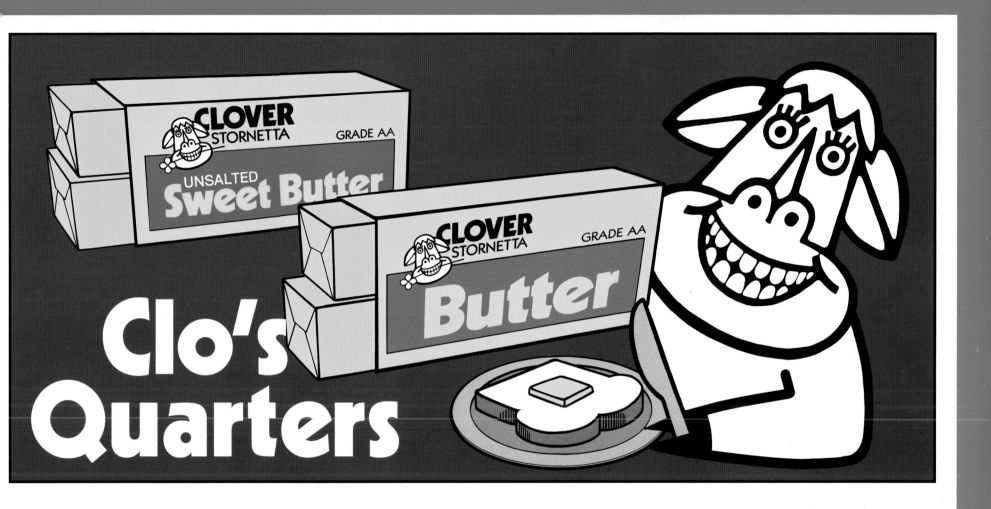

Clo's Quarters

1986

31

Clo's look

"Clo's look" and "New designer Clos" were part of the campaign to introduce a new package design for Clover products, for the first time, including illustrations of Clo.

1986

New designer Clos

Clover-Stornetta Farms

My Fair Lady
Sonoma County Fair

July 27 - August 9

Santa Rosa

This board helped promote the Sonoma County Fair, and called attention to one of the Fair's prime attractions, the Clover ice cream booth, where patrons could beat the heat with free ice cream cones.

Wolfgang Amadeus Moozart

Always ready to promote culture, Clo offered some of the great composer's piano music on this board.
The music could actually be heard as part of a TV commercial that combined animation and live action,
bringing the billboard to life.

1987

Funny, Clo doesn't look 75!

Great dairy products since 1913

The Clover brand name celebrated its 75th Anniversary!

Half Galleon

Clo rides the high seas on one of three billboards brought to life, combining animation and live action, for a TV commercial. The skill of animator Damon Rarey showed Clo firing her cannon across the bow of Gene and Dan Benedetti's passing convertible.

1988

Christopher Cowlumbus in the Moo World

Miss Sonoma Cownty

van Clo's favorite pitcher

Note van Clo's left ear. The original painting by van Clo still exists.

Tip Clo through your two lips

The headline for this board won the top prize in a 1989 contest that drew 7,481 billboard ideas. Ally Minatta of Sonoma was the winner.

Splendor in the glass

Second prize in the 1989 contest went to Helen Vanderbilt of San Anselmo for this headline.

Here's lickin' at you, kid.

This board was also brought to life as a TV commercial, featuring Clo on a foggy runway in Casablanca, ready to share some Clover Ice Cream.

1990

Moona Lisa

A classic pitcher.

A perfect classic.

Clo's visions are an effective and entertaining way to sell Clover's excellent product.

The famed poster by Toulouse-Lautrec provided the multi-talented Clo with an opportunity to demonstrate her skill as a high-kicking cancan dancer.

1991

Moooy bueno

It's not Clover 'til the fat lady sings!

Again demonstrating Clo's dedication to the arts, everyone's favorite cow performs in grand opera as the star soprano, probably in an opus by Wagner.

1992

Clo's Friends

The sharks are circling on this one.

The Greatest Clo on Earth

The gardens of Giverny could be anywhere.

1993

Clover was a forerunner of recycling, done in conjunction with a national recycling effort.

1993

Clo commemorates the 50th Anniversary of "D" Day.

Her Moojesty

Clo was the reigning queen of hearts at the Renaissance Faire at Black Point, in Novato, California.

1994

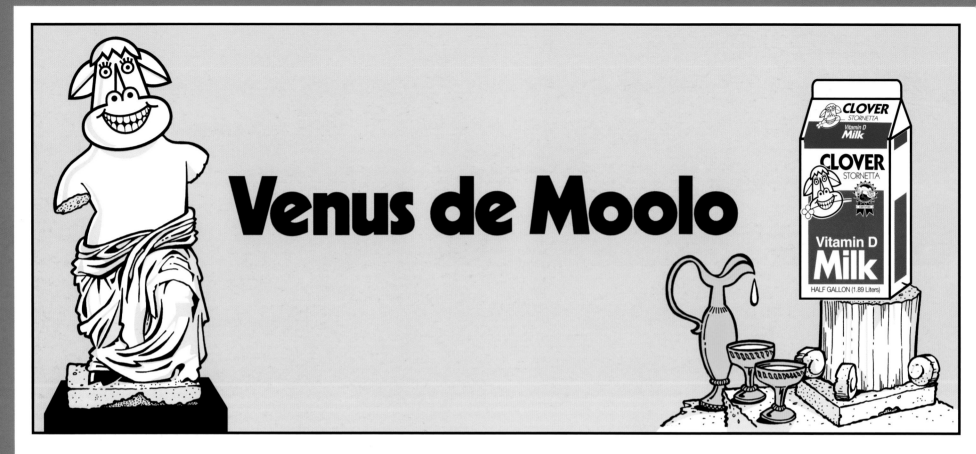

Venus de Moolo

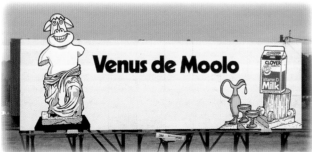

Clo's next encownter with Marine World.

Moovin' right along...

Clo's call

Expressway Exit for Crushers Baseball

Clo shows up as the umpire at a Crushers game, a local professional baseball team, where she calls the team's mascot, the Abominable Sonoman, safe at home.

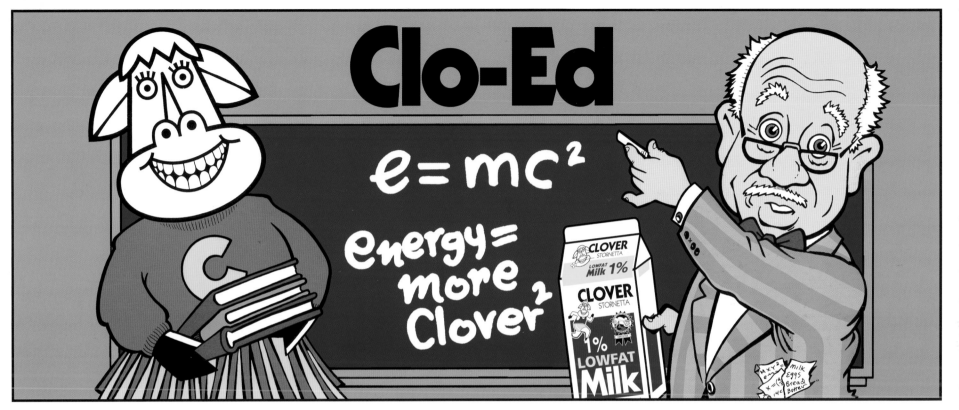

Clo's theory of extraordinary milk.

1995

Anthony & Clopatra

Anthony and Clopatra

Scooper Bowl

Celebrating another '49ers trip to the Super Bowl,
Clo demonstrates her passing prowess with an ice cream scoop.

19584A

Clo is a daredevil flyer in this adventure scene.

Clo's hangar

1996

Mooby Dick

Clo's vintage herds appeared in both Napa and Sonoma counties.

Dairy Godmother

This board is the one and only without our Clo.

Cloverland Express

Clo won her very own gold during the 1996 Summer Olympics.

Clo's inspection

Clover Stornetta Farms had embarked upon a public relations move to promote their North Coast Excellence Program, which proclaimed their philosophy of extraordinarily high standards for their milk. This included bacteria and coliform counts far lower than state and federal standards, and the decision not to include bovine growth hormone (rBST), now banned in Canada, Europe, and Clover, but allowed in the United States.

CLOreogHEIFER

Clo trimmed some 150 pounds off her buxom frame during her short-lived but satisfying career as a dancer and personal trainer.

1996

Quart
Jester

1997
78

Clo White and the seven Quarts

"Clo White" is a favorite of Clo's public. During its development process, it had a record-breaking amount of toadstool revisions.

Clo and Marine World (before it was Six Flags), promote healthy food and entertainment together.

1997

Mt. Rushmoooer

A perfect board!

Cowpernicus & the Milky Way

As in all the billboards, the agency researched history to make sure "Cowpernicus" was appropriately attired, and with the correct instruments. Though originally we thought Cowpernicus would have a telescope, we discovered that at that time, they had not been invented. Instead, Cowpernicus was equipped with an historically correct sextant.

1997

Clover again joined up with Six Flags New Marine World Theme Park.

1998

Edgar Allan Clo

This is considered a quintessential Clo billboard: simple, direct, with elegance in costume and composition. There was much discussion about her mustache, and it changed from white to black, and back to white again. Early in the creative process, she also had a mane of black hair, but that was discarded along the way.

1998

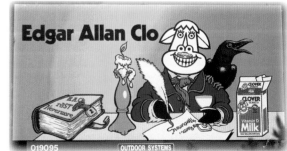

019095   OUTDOOR SYSTEMS

Fiddler on the Hoof

Tradition.

In what other boards does Clo sport a head of hair?

Clo's Knit Family

One of Clover's favorites, "Clo's Knit Family" epitomizes the philosophy Clover Stornetta nurtures towards their customers, employees, and products.

1999

Sears Point Raceway and Clo join up for the first time to enjoy the need for speed: fast food and fast fun.

Eclological

Our favorite bovine shows her devotion to ecology, as she introduces Clover's line of organic milk.

1999

Clo ushered in the new millennium with more dimensional graphics, but kept her perfectly adorable cartoon physique...a cartoon!

1999

Clover the Rainbow

We know, the slippers aren't ruby-red, and we couldn't say "Somewhere"!

The Sound of Moosic

"Sound of Moosic" was a billboard destined to happen, often-suggested by many fans. We were happy to compose it.

The color of the cliffs and water was changed three times.

Mooovin' at Sears Point

Sears Point really got into the spirit of Clo, suggesting both the headline and Clo's spotted car.

Udderly Striking

Clover welcomed 8,000 members of the Women's Bowling League into Sonoma County with this smashing billboard.

This is Clo in her perfect state: sensitive, thoughtful, and naked. We always knew she was an artistic feat, but a cross between Descartes and Rodin? You go, girl! Please stay in our hearts forever.